CONTENTS

BELIEFS

SEEKING A REFUGE

'You are the master, you are the refuge.' [Dhammapada 25] Buddha images in Thailand

BUDDHISM

Lilian Weatherley

Religious Education Adviser for the Diocese of Winchester

SERIES EDITOR: CLIVE ERRICKER

Lecturer in Arts Education
University of Warwick

About the Themes in Religion series

This series of books offers a lively and accessible introduction to the six main world religions for students taking GCSE Religious Studies. The books can be used separately to study one religious tradition, or they can be used together, to investigate one theme across the traditions, such as beliefs, worship, pilgrimage or values. The section on values shows how each religion reacts to everyday life and the modern world. The spreads offer class activities and assignments that relate to coursework requirements and encourage further research, and each book provides a glossary of important terms and a reading list.

Each spread is self-contained and presents an important aspect of each religion. Through carefully chosen photographs, clear text and relevant quotations from scriptures and believers, students will learn about each religion and the living impact it has for believers today. The wide variety of assignments help pupils to evaluate what they have read, suggest activities to further their understanding, and raise issues for them to reflect on.

We hope that these books will provide students of all abilities with a stimulating introduction to these religions, and that the enjoyment of using them matches that of producing them.

Clive Erricker

Thank You
I would like to thank the following for their kind help and support: Lois Sayle, Adrian Abbots, Abhaya, and Ajahn Anando from Chithurst Forest Monastery.

About Buddhism

'We are what we think
All that we are arises with our thoughts
With our thoughts we make the world.'
[Dhammapada 1]

During the last twenty years an increased interest in Buddhism in the West has resulted in many students wishing to study this major world faith for GCSE. This involves the rethinking of established Western ideas and coming to terms with one of the central issues of Buddhism – mental training. Students of Buddhism will need to develop an awareness and understanding of Buddhist thought so that they can begin to see the world through the eyes of a Buddhist and evaluate issues of everyday life from a Buddhist viewpoint.

This book, through its photographs, quotations, text and assignments, offers students the opportunity to gain a step-by-step insight into what it means to be a Buddhist in today's society.

Lilian Weatherley

Notes: The language of the traditions, which is usually one of the biggest hurdles for the student, is set in context. Pali is generally used for the Theravada tradition and Sanskrit for the Mahayana. The Buddhist terms are explained in a clear and simple way.

In the Beliefs section the life of the monastic Sangha is illustrated through a Theravada example to avoid over-complication. Later in the book examples of Mahayana practice are referred to. We hope teachers will bear this in mind when using it with pupils and note that this does not imply any priority is given to either.

For Stephen

A refuge is a shelter in times of difficulty. Sometimes it is a place, but it can also be a teaching, or someone you trust and turn to for help and guidance. Buddhists put their trust in **Three Refuges**:

> To the Buddha I go for refuge.
> To the Dhamma I go for refuge.
> To the Sangha I go for refuge.

This is recited daily and is at the heart of Buddhist belief. These refuges are so precious that they are often called the **Three Jewels** or the Triple Gem.

A prince is born

We begin our study of Buddhism with the legend of a young prince whose life led him on a journey to become a **Buddha** or 'enlightened one'.

The place is India and the date about 563 BCE. Queen Mahamaya, the wife of King Suddhodana, was troubled by a dream. Wise men interpreted this to mean that the queen was to have a son who would one day become a great man, either a king or a **sadhu** (a holy man who gives up all worldly things).

Later that year Prince **Siddhattha Gotama** was born. He grew to be handsome and intelligent but the king became worried by his son's gentleness. Would this child succeed him as a warrior or would he become a sadhu?

More responsibility was the answer.

Siddhattha must have a wife. A family would ensure that he remained in the palace. The beautiful Princess Yasodhara was chosen and the two were married. When later the princess gave birth to a son the old king was delighted.

As time passed Siddhattha began to feel discontented and decided to visit the unknown kingdom outside the palace walls.

Three times he journeyed outside and each time he witnessed tragedies that he had not seen before: an old man, a sick man, and a corpse. Then he made a fourth journey. This time he met a sadhu who was searching to find the true meaning of life.

'I too shall give up my wealth and leave my home to find a solution to suffering,' thought Siddhattha.

The king tried to stop his son, but one night while all in the palace slept, Siddhattha made his difficult decision and left the palace to begin his search.

ASSIGNMENTS

- Write the letter that Siddhattha might have written to his father explaining the reasons for his decision and why the palace was no longer a refuge.

- Write a reply from the king questioning Siddhattha's decision and judgement.

- Act out the final conversation that might have taken place between Siddhattha and his father if the king had found his son leaving.

KEY WORDS

Three Refuges   Three Jewels
Buddha   sadhu   Siddhattha Gotama

THE BUDDHA

Siddhattha's search

Once out of the palace gates the prince exchanged his silk robes for those of a sadhu. He cut off his hair and handed his jewels to his servant to take back to the palace.

For many years Siddhattha wandered the forests. He met famous religious teachers, but they gave him no solution to his problem. He tried fasting and self-denial, but without success.

> All my limbs became like the knotted joints of withered creepers, my buttocks like a bullock's hoof, my protruding backbone like a string of balls, my gaunt ribs like the crazy rafters of a tumbledown shed. My eyes lay deep in their sockets, their pupils sparkling like waters in a deep well.
>
> [Middle Length Sayings 245]

One evening, Siddhattha remembered how as a child he would sit under a tree in the palace garden to think over his problems. He decided to make a cushion of grass and sit under a tree, vowing, 'I shall not stir from this seat until I have gained absolute insight.'

His task was not easy. He was alone, but the evil demon Mara was there to tempt him away from his quest. Finally,

through self-sacrifice and meditation, he triumphed. He had overthrown temptation and discovered the way to end suffering. He was **Enlightened**. He was a Buddha.

> Such was the vision, the knowledge, the wisdom, the science, the light, that arose in me with regard to things not heard before.
>
> [Kindred Sayings 56]

Have you ever been tempted?

● The picture shows the Buddha being tempted at the moment of Enlightenment. What do you think these temptations might have been? Discuss them with a partner and see if you can fit them under these five headings:
Doubt, Lustful Desire, Worry, Laziness, Ill Will or Anger.

These are what Buddhists call the **Five Hindrances** and they are major obstacles on the way to enlightenment.

> When these Five Hindrances have been put away within him, he looks upon himself as freed from debt, rid of disease, out of jail, a free man and secure.
>
> [Dialogues of the Buddha 11]

ASSIGNMENTS

● Siddhattha was able to triumph over temptation. What qualities do you think he possessed that made this possible? Discuss this in class then summarise the various ideas in your own words.

● Write newspaper reports to go with the following headlines:
  a) Callous young prince abandons wife and family
  b) Compassionate young prince leaves the palace and discovers a cure for suffering

Share your two reports with a partner. Discuss how they show the various ways in which we take refuge in things.

● Look at the way the Buddha has been depicted on page 4 then write down four reasons why you think Buddhists feel able to put their trust in this man and his achievement.

KEY WORDS

Enlightened   Five Hindrances

The attack of Mara

THE DHAMMA

> The Dhamma is the language of the heart.

Siddhatta discovered that life is not always satisfactory. We all experience pain and suffering. Sometimes this is physical pain but often it is mental pain and heartache. Once enlightened he offered a solution to life's problems in his teachings or **Dhamma** – the second of the Three Refuges. He had diagnosed the problem and now, like a doctor, he was able to offer a prescription and cure. This he called the **Four Noble Truths**.

The diagnosis

Look at the world around you. It is not difficult to find examples of suffering and unsatisfactoriness. This is the *first* Noble Truth – **Dukkha** – realising and accepting that suffering and unsatisfactoriness exist.

● Make a collection of newspaper cuttings that show suffering and unsatisfactoriness. Now pick out one that makes you feel that life is unsatisfactory and write down the reasons for your choice.

The Buddha saw that there are three aspects of Dukkha, which he called the **Three Marks of Existence**:

Dukkha: The feeling of unsatisfactoriness
Anicca: Realising that nothing is permanent
Anatta: Understanding that if nothing is permanent then we have no permanent self

We have explored the first aspect. Now let us look at Anicca and Anatta.

Anicca

Think of some changes that are taking place around you. It might be a change in fashion, landscape or nature. This impermanence Buddhists call **Anicca**. Look at the photographs. Are they the same person? What do you think the verse in the caption is saying?

'For behold your body –
A painted puppet, a toy,
Jointed and sick and full of false imaginings
A shadow that shifts and fades.'
[Dhammapada 11]

Anatta

● Find photos of yourself at different ages. Are you the same person that you were when you were two years old? How have you changed? Discuss this with a partner.

If things around us are constantly changing then so are we. A Buddhist would say we are like foam in a bubble bath, changing from moment to moment.

> Understand that the body
> Is merely the foam of a wave
> The shadow of a shadow
>
> [Dhammapada 4]

If we are are changing in this way, do 'we' exist? A Buddhist would say that 'we' do not. This is **Anatta**: no self.

Our bodies are made up of many parts, called aggregates or **khandhas**, just like the particles of broken stone that make up concrete. They fall into five categories: Matter – Feelings – Perception – Mental Activities – Consciousness. These come together at birth, they are constantly changing, and then they disintegrate when we die.

ASSIGNMENTS

● Using your photographs and the newspaper cuttings you have collected, *either* write a few paragraphs or a poem to explain the word 'Dukkha', *or* create a collage with the title 'Dukkha' and write a short commentary about your picture.

● 'All things are impermanent.' Debate this in class and write up the two sides of the argument.

KEY WORDS

Dhamma   Four Noble Truths
Dukkha   Three Marks of Existence
Anicca   Anatta   khandhas

WHY DOES SUFFERING EXIST?

The *second* Noble Truth is **Samudaya** – the origin of suffering and unsatisfactoriness. The Buddha taught that because everything is constantly changing so are our desires.

● Think back to your early childhood. Were there things that you desperately wanted? A doll's pram or a train set? Do you still want these things? Write down five things that you would like at this moment. Will you still want them in 10 years' time?

As human beings we have a desire and thirst to cling on to life and material possessions. This thirst is called **Tanha** and it is the reason why suffering (Dukkha) exists. We suffer through our greed, hatred and ignorance, wanting things we cannot have.

● Tibetan Buddhists use three creatures to symbolise greed, hatred and ignorance. Look at the central circle in the picture, can you guess which one is which?

The fool is his own enemy
Seeking wealth he destroys himself.

[Dhammapada 24]

The pig is ignorance, the snake hatred and the cockerel greed. Each one chases the other in a never-ending circle which represents **Samsara**, the endless cycle of existence: birth, death and rebirth.

A Tibetan Wheel of Life

The prescription and cure

The Buddha saw that it is only when we are able to remove our greed, hatred and ignorance that we can begin to remove suffering. This is the *third* Noble Truth – **Nirodha** – letting go of suffering.

Think again about something that you desperately wanted but couldn't have. If you hadn't wanted it so badly in the beginning, you wouldn't have been so disappointed when you didn't receive it.

Weeds choke the field,
Passion poisons the nature of man,
And hatred, ignorance and desire.
Honour the man who is without
Passion, hatred, ignorance and desire.

[Dhammapada 24]

ASSIGNMENTS

● Read the quotations from the Dhammapada and think about ways in which greed, hatred and ignorance cause suffering in the world. Then prepare a two-minute radio broadcast on greed, hatred and ignorance in the world today. Talk about how they arise and what the Buddhist viewpoint is.

● Imagine you are a Buddhist, and a non-Buddhist friend asks you why you think suffering exists. Write the dialogue between you.

KEY WORDS

Samudaya   Tanha   Samsara
Nirodha

THE NOBLE EIGHTFOLD PATH

The boat in the picture is being tossed about on a stormy sea. To the Buddhist, human beings are like the people in that boat setting out on the voyage of Samsara. Sometimes the journey is calm and peaceful, but often it is stormy and turbulent. A way out of the troubled waters and into the calm is the *fourth* Noble Truth – **Magga**, the Middle Way of the **Noble Eightfold Path**. The eight steps of the path can be divided into three groups: Morality, Concentration and Wisdom.

● Think carefully about how your life would change if you tried to follow these eight steps. Share your thoughts with a partner.

Right Concentration
To remain free from all mental disturbances such as worry, envy and anxiety.
(CONCENTRATION)

Right Viewpoint
Being able to see and understand things as they really are – as unsatisfactory.
(WISDOM)

Right Intention
Often called Right Thought. Being able to direct thoughts in an unselfish way.
(MORALITY)

Right Mindfulness
Being able to be aware of all you do in thought and action from moment to moment.
(CONCENTRATION)

The Noble Eightfold Path

Right Speech
To abstain from lying, gossiping or speaking unthoughtfully.
(MORALITY)

Right Effort
Making an effort to be mindful of the way things are.
(CONCENTRATION)

Right Livelihood
To maintain a living or job that avoids harmfulness.
(MORALITY)

Right Action
To behave in a way that will not bring suffering to others.
(MORALITY)

By following the path a person might achieve **Nibbana** (**Nirvana** in Sanskrit), a state of bliss free from suffering and unsatisfactoriness. Like a ship's steering wheel the path guides us over the water, giving direction. It is a Middle Way that avoids extremes.

The parable of the raft

The Buddha's teaching is like the boat in the picture. It helps as a guide across the water to the other shore and gives us an ideal to work towards. It is not the truth itself, but an aid to finding the truth. The Buddha explained this in the parable of the raft:

A man going along a highway might see a great stretch of water, the near bank dangerous and frightening but the far bank safe and secure. As there is not a boat nor a bridge for crossing, it occurs to the man to build a raft from sticks, branches and foliage. Once across the river he wonders if he should carry the raft with him on his journey or submerge it under water. The Dhamma is like the raft, to be used for crossing over, not for retaining.

[Middle Length Sayings 22]

'Go beyond, this way or that,
to the farther shore, here the world
dissolves and everything becomes clear.'
[Dhammapada 26]

Ajahn Sumedho, a Buddhist monk, helps us to understand the parable:

> Religious traditions are all based on doing good, refraining from doing evil. Therefore, if one clings to them, then one is bound to them. If one regards religion as just a convention, then one can learn how to use it properly. It is the raft that takes one across.

ASSIGNMENTS

● Write a pamphlet for a young child explaining the Eightfold Path. Try to illustrate each of the steps.

● Produce an article for a magazine showing how a particular world situation might improve if people began to follow the Eightfold Path.

KEY WORDS

Magga   Noble Eightfold Path
Nibbana   Nirvana

THE SANGHA

The word **Sangha** means 'community', and it is the third of the Three Refuges. It consists of the monks, the nuns and the lay people – ordinary Buddhists – although it is often used to refer simply to the monks. The Buddha said that in the relationship between the monk and the man who lives with his family each was to be dependent on the other.

Lay Buddhists

The picture shows Lois, a lay Buddhist. I asked her what it meant to be a Buddhist and why she felt able to put her trust in the Buddha and to recite the Three Refuges:

'I put my trust in the Buddha when I realised the truth of his teaching. Buddhism has provided me with a way of living which I find gives me great peace and happiness. I try to follow the Buddhist precepts, which provide a practical framework for everyday living. Making the effort to live by these precepts has made me explore my attitudes and actions.'

You will see that Lois talks about the **precepts**. The word means 'moral instructions', but in Buddhism they are not strict commands. They are more like a target that you are aiming for. Sometimes you might miss, but the important thing is to aspire towards them or to keep trying.

The precepts

The precepts come under 'Right Action' in the Eightfold Path, and as a lay Buddhist Lois is required to follow five of them:

To refrain from injuring living things.
To refrain from taking that which is not given.
To refrain from sexual immorality.
To refrain from false or malicious speech.
To refrain from taking intoxicating drink and drugs.

● Would you find it easy to follow these precepts? Which one would you find most difficult? Discuss this with a partner.

A novice sweeps the ground at a monastery in Thailand. How would he apply the first precept to this action?

The boy above is a novice or **samanera**. In some South Asian countries boys often enter a monastery for a short period. They help with the running of the monastery, study Buddhist teaching and follow an additional five precepts:

Not to eat at inappropriate times (not to indulge in food).
To abstain from singing, dancing and acting (not to seek distraction through entertainment).
Not to use garlands, ornaments and perfume.
Not to sleep in a high or broad bed (not to indulge in sleep).
Not to receive gold or silver (money).

● Would you find these easier or more difficult to keep than the first five?

ASSIGNMENTS

● Try to keep the first five precepts for a day or two and then write a diary entry to say how well you succeeded or failed.

● Write your own list of precepts for society today. Are any of them the same as the Buddhist precepts? Pick out the ones that are similar and then design a poster explaining their relevance to modern life.

KEY WORDS

Sangha   precepts   samanera

MONKS AND NUNS

At the heart of the Sangha are the monks – **bhikkhus,** and nuns – **bhikkhunis.** Ajahn

Anando is a Buddhist monk in Britain who belongs to an order of monks from Thailand.

One who shares

When Siddhattha gave up his princely status he became an almsman, living on gifts (alms) that were offered to him. The monks continue this tradition, relying on the lay community for gifts of food, clothing and shelter.

'Bhikkhu' means 'one who lives on alms'. Each day monks go out on their almsround to collect their daily food from the local community. They are not allowed to ask for food and so without the lay people monasteries would not survive. The lay people in turn benefit from the presence of monks and their teaching.

When Ajahn Anando was in Thailand he also went out on the daily almsround to collect his food, but in countries where there is not a strong Buddhist tradition it may be necessary for the lay Buddhists to go to the monastery to prepare the meal for the monks.

This is the only meal of the day for monks. It is called the **dana**, which means 'giving'. It must be collected, received and consumed between dawn and noon.

● Why are the monks not allowed to *ask* for food?

I asked Ajahn Anando why he became a bhikkhu:

'I first became interested in Buddhism through reading about it while I was at university. I realised that I had been thinking as a Buddhist for a long time. I felt very much at home with Buddhism.

I found it both inspiring and attractive, and it has kept my interest throughout the years. I could only read about Buddhism for so long, however, and eventually it became obvious that I had to practise it. The essential aspect of Buddhism is meditation practice and I eventually had the opportunity to do some while I was in India.

There I saw it was what I needed, although it demanded a degree of self-discipline that was beyond me at the time. Then I went to Thailand and met a Buddhist monk. This gave me an opportunity to see what it was like for a few weeks until I took the precepts as a novice. I discovered it was actually very much what I was looking for. I could put my trust in the Buddha because his teaching gave me direction. Now, 18 years later, it is still a source of inspiration and joy for me.'

ASSIGNMENTS

● 'He who with trusting heart takes a Buddha as his guide, and the Truth and the Order.'

Write a booklet to explain this quotation. You may need to look back through the chapter on 'Beliefs' to help you.

● Write down one question you would like to ask Ajahn Anando and explain why. (Ajahn means 'teacher' in Thai.)

KEY WORDS

bhikkhu   bhikkhuni   dana

BECOMING A MONK

In the days of the Buddha, men became monks by taking part in a simple acceptance ceremony. The Buddha ordained the monks by saying:

'Come bhikkhu, well-expounded is the Dhamma. Live a chaste life for the complete end of suffering.'

As the numbers of followers grew, it was no longer possible for the Buddha himself to ordain everyone. So the responsibility for ordination fell to senior monks. It was agreed that in a country where there were many monks, ten should be present for an ordination to take place, but in places outside the Ganges valley five would be sufficient.

The ceremony developed into two main parts: lower ordination as a samanera,

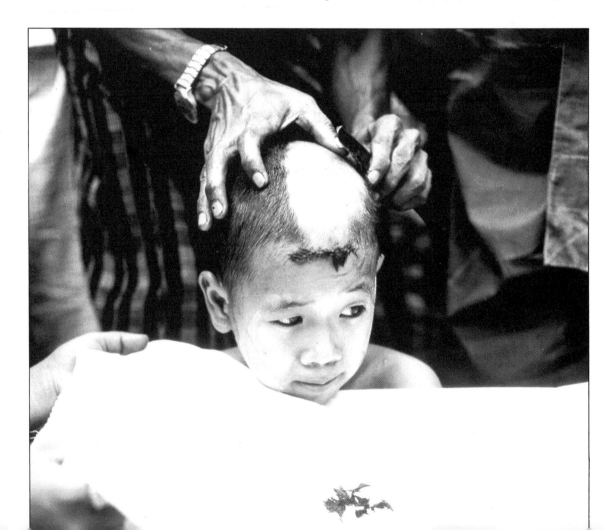

which took place between the ages of eight and twenty, and higher ordination to bhikkhu for men over twenty.

Gradually women were also allowed to be ordained as nuns (bhikkhunis), but the numbers have remained small.

Lower ordination

Siddhattha cut off his hair when he left the palace to become a holy man. The boy in the photograph is also having his head shaved as a sign that he is renouncing his previous life and preparing for samanera ordination. During this ceremony the boy will recite the Three Refuges and then take the Ten Precepts.

At Ajahn Anando's monastery men and women can become novices over the age of twenty. They take eight precepts and are given the title of anagarika.

● Can you think of any other religious traditions in which the head is shaved?

Higher ordination

The candidates for higher ordination are asked four questions: Are they free from disease, debt, and other commitments, and do they have their parents' permission?

'Let him who desires to receive ordination first have his hair and beard cut off.' [Vinaya Pitaka]

Once this has been established the ceremony continues and the candidates receive their almsbowls and a set of robes: an under robe, an outer robe, and an upper robe.

A bhikkhu, considering wisely, makes use of his robes – only to keep off the cold, to keep off heat, to keep off gadflies, mosquitoes, winds and the sun and creeping creatures and to cover himself decently.

[Middle Length Sayings]

The Burmese boy in the photograph will put on the traditional saffron robes worn by the wandering holy men in the days of Siddhattha. The colour symbolised immortality. Originally they would have been made from rags that had been sewn together and dyed. The colour of the robes varies depending on the Buddhist tradition. All ordained Theravada monks wear saffron, Tibetan monks wear maroon and Japanese Zen monks wear black.

ASSIGNMENTS

● Imagine that you are a Buddhist boy who has just become a samanera. Using these pages and some of the books on page 64, write a diary entry explaining what happened and how you felt.

● Do you think a person's past life should influence their suitability for acceptance as a monk? If so, what questions would you ask a prospective candidate? Include the qualities that you think are important for someone wishing to become a Buddhist monk.

LIFE AS A MONK

● If you were asked to give up all you possess except eight items, what would you choose? Make a list then compare it with a partner's.

The picture shows the eight items that a Theravada monk was originally allowed to possess: three robes, a waistband, an almsbowl, a razor, a needle and a water-strainer.

As circumstances change, other small items are occasionally permitted, but these must be plain and simple. One example today would be a pen.

The Vinaya

● Most institutions have rules of some kind. Write down five of your school rules. Can you think of a reason why they were introduced?

During the early years of Buddhism, rules and regulations for control of the Sangha were simple, but as the numbers of monks and nuns increased so a code of discipline, or **Vinaya**, was agreed and written down.

The precepts are part of the Vinaya, but

monks and nuns have further rules to help them live with clear and happy minds. Here are some rules from Ajahn Anando's monastery:

A bhikkhu lives on the food that he is offered.

No bhikkhu may eat fruit or vegetables containing fertile seeds unless the seeds have been removed or the fruit has been made allowable by being slightly damaged with a knife.

Three robes only are permitted but it is accepted that in cold climates these can be supplemented by sweaters, socks, etc.

The bhikkhu must not sleep in the same room more than three nights with an unordained male.

The bhikkhu must not lie down in the same room as a female.

Oral medicines must only be used if they are offered in the same way as food.

Medicines are those things that are specifically for illness.

The Western Buddhist Order

In 1968 a new movement of Buddhism, called the Western Buddhist Order, began in Britain. The Order believes that many of these traditional rules are out of date because they have not adapted to modern-day circumstances. A member of the Order explains:

'Sometimes traditions of long standing lose the ability to distinguish between what is essential and what is an expression of local or national culture. I chose to join the Western Buddhist Order because it freely draws on traditional Buddhism for inspiration while leaving behind its Eastern cultural wrappings ... I am not wearing robes and I don't have a shaven head ... For us the monk's yellow robe is strange and exotic. Perhaps Buddhist monks in the West should all wear faded blue jeans and an old jumper. That would be closer to the Buddhism of the Buddha's time.'

ASSIGNMENTS

● From your knowledge and understanding of Buddhism explain why it is possible to adapt the Vinaya to suit the changing circumstances. Then write a conversation that might take place between a traditional Theravada bhikkhu and a member of the Western Buddhist Order.

● Write a letter to your parents requesting their permission for you to become a Buddhist monk. Explain the reasons for your decision and give them an idea of what life will be like for you.

● Imagine you are a newspaper reporter and that you have been given the task of writing an article about your local Buddhist community explaining its way of life. You could find out if there is one near you, or use some of the books listed on page 64. Write the article.

KEY WORDS

Vinaya

SCRIPTURES

FROM THE VOICE TO THE PEN

After a ministry of 45 years the Buddha died at the age of 80. He had then entered a state of **Parinibbana**, physical death and final release from Samsara.

There was no successor but the Buddha's teachings lived on. They had been memorised by his followers and were passed on by word of mouth, for three or four centuries.

Different ships on the same journey

As time passed, some of the Buddha's teachings became changed or elaborated, so in 480 BCE a council of the faithful was called at Rajgir. It was attended by the Buddha's closest friends and followers who tried to recollect the exact words of the Buddha. After some debate, a definitive version was finally agreed and given to specialists to learn by heart.

This oral tradition continued and eventually the words became translated into local languages. By 380 BCE it was felt that in some regions the monks were becoming lax about the Vinaya rules and so a second council was called at Vesali.

During this second council a difference of opinion arose over the correct interpretation of the Buddha's teaching. One group refused to accept the decision of the council and left the meeting. The monks who remained became known as the Elders.

The two main schools

This split within the monks was to remain. After many centuries the two main schools of Buddhism emerged: the **Mahayana** or Great Vehicle, and the **Theravada**, meaning 'way of the elders', and sometimes known by the derogatory term of **Hinayana** or Lesser Vehicle.

Mahayana Buddhism spread northwards through Nepal into Tibet, China, Japan, Mongolia, Korea and Vietnam. Sometimes called the Northern School it includes Tibetan Buddhism, Pure Land and Zen.

Theravada Buddhism spread southwards from India into Sri Lanka, Burma, Thailand, Cambodia and Laos.

The Theravada scriptures

It is said that the first Buddhist scriptures were finally written down by the Theravada monks at a fourth council. This was held in Sri Lanka during the first century BCE. Using the ancient Indian language of Pali, the words which had been memorised by the elders for so long were eventually transferred to palm leaves, four centuries after the Buddha's death. This collection of writings became known as the Pali Canon, or Tipitaka.

ASSIGNMENTS

● Try to remember an important event from your childhood. With a partner tell each other your stories. Try to memorise your partner's story and then write it down. Think carefully about what you write and how you could preserve this story for future generations. You could compile a class anthology.

● Draw a map of the countries mentioned. Colour in which countries adopted Mahayana or Theravada Buddhism.

KEY WORDS

Parinibbana   Mahayana   Theravada
Hinayana

'Here are the words of the teacher who is gone.'
[Dialogues of the Buddha] A monastery in Burma

THE PALI CANON

Buddhists believe that to preserve the quality of the Pali Canon it was divided into three sections and stored in three baskets or **Tipitaka**: the Vinaya Pitaka, the Sutta Pitaka and the Abhidhamma Pitaka.

The Vinaya Pitaka

In this basket of discipline we find the 227 rules and regulations for the monks and the nuns. Here are some examples:

> I shall eat the alms-food carefully.
> I shall eat the alms-food as it comes without making exceptions.
> I shall not hide sauces and curries with rice in order to get more.

● How do you think this relates to the dana meal? Look back at page 17 and discuss your ideas.

The Sutta Pitaka

The word **sutta** ('sutra' in Sanskrit) means 'thread'. In this basket we find some of the oldest teachings and sayings of the Buddha: the Four Noble Truths, the Eightfold Path, and some of the most popular Buddhist literature, including the Dhammapada and the Jataka tales.

The Dhammapada, or Path of Truth, is a collection of the Buddha's sayings which were written down between 563 and 483 BCE. These have become an important source of guidance for Buddhists everywhere, but especially in Sri Lanka and elsewhere in Southern Asia.

The Jataka tales are a collection of stories about the Buddha's previous lives. They encourage the **Ten Perfections** which lead to perfect Buddhahood: generosity, virtue, renunciation, wisdom, energy, patience, truthfulness, resolution, loving kindness and an even temper. Here is one of the stories, called 'The Patient Buffalo':

> A huge buffalo lay asleep under a tree, when a mischievous monkey saw him and chanted: 'I know a good old buffalo, who's sleeping 'neath the tree, but I am not afraid of him, nor he afraid of me.'
>
> Then the little monkey began tormenting the buffalo, trying all sorts of tricks to make the beast angry. He even tried tickling his ears, but the buffalo took no notice.
>
> One day a fairy appeared and asked, 'Why do you let this monkey torment you so? You are strong enough to stop him.'
>
> 'The monkey is small', said the buffalo, 'and has a small brain. Why should I make him suffer so that I can be happy.'

'My children, I have not come now among you as your Buddha for the first time. I have come many times before. Sometimes as a child among children, sometimes among the animals as one of their kind.'
[Jataka tales]

● Read the story of the Patient Buffalo. Can you find the Buddha? What teachings do you think the Buddha is giving in this story?

ASSIGNMENTS

● Write a paragraph explaining why you think Theravada Buddhists have called the second basket the *Sutta* Pitaka.

● Design a leaflet that will help Buddhist children understand the contents of the Tipitaka.

● Using the caption, try to write your own 'Jataka tale' on the theme of truthfulness.

The Abhidhamma Pitaka

This basket contained the Higher Teachings. They are divided into seven books that are a psychology of Buddhist teaching and were intended for specialists rather than the ordinary people. They examine in questions and answers the key teachings of the Buddha.

KEY WORDS

Tipitaka   sutta   Ten Perfections

THE MAHAYANA SCRIPTURES

As Buddhism spread so other ideas and scriptures developed. (Indian Mahayana scriptures were written in Sanskrit not Pali, so there are variations in spelling, such as 'sutra' for 'sutta', 'nirvana' for 'nibbana', 'Dharma' for 'Dhamma'.)

In these writings the figure of Siddhattha (or Siddhartha) began to take on a more mystical and poetic look. Mahayana

Buddhists came to believe that he was not the only Buddha that the world had known. There had been many before him and there would be others in the future.

With this idea came a belief in a new celestial being called a **bodhisattva**. 'Bodhi' means 'enlightenment' and 'sattva' means 'essence'. A bodhisattva is an enlightened being who delays Nirvana in

order to keep in contact with humans. This being is capable of renouncing everything, including enlightenment and Buddhahood, in order to return to the world with true compassion to help others along the path.

> A bodhisattva who is not attached to anything when he gives, like a person in the daylight who can see things as they really are.
>
> [Diamond Sutra]

The Prajnaparamita Sutras

These **sutras** were written in Sanskrit between 100 BCE and 600 CE. They are a guide to perfect wisdom or **Prajna**, the wisdom of the bodhisattva. A bodhisattva has a perfect wisdom which goes beyond the wisdom of the world. This wisdom fully understands the absence of self, which is called **Sunyata**, or emptiness.

> In emptiness there is no form, nor feeling, nor perception, nor impulse, nor consciousness; no eye, ear, nose, tongue, body, mind; no forms, sounds, smells, tastes, touchables or objects of mind; no sight-organ element, and so forth until we come to no mind-consciousness element.
>
> [Heart Sutra 5]

In the early days of Buddhism, chanting was more common than silent reading. Monks would take one or two sutras and learn them by heart, often chanting them up to 30 times a day. Some scriptures became very popular, and the Diamond and Heart Sutras were regarded as two of the holiest of the Prajnaparamita Sutras. They both describe the role of the bodhisattva.

> If a bodhisattva has any notion of a being, a person, or a self, he could not be called a bodhisattva. A bodhisattva should not give a gift while basing himself on the notion of form, sound, smell, taste, touch, or while basing himself on any thought. He should give without the notion of a giver or a gift. That great being who gives without basing himself on any notion, his merit is not easy to measure.
>
> [Diamond Sutra 3]

ASSIGNMENTS

- The bodhisattva in the picture is Avalokiteshvara, the bodhisattva of great compassion. He has 1,000 arms, with an eye on each hand. How do you think he represents the qualities of Perfect Wisdom and Compassion?
- Write down your own definition of 'wisdom' then look back at the quotations on this page. How would you answer the question 'What is Wisdom?' from a Mahayana Buddhist point of view? Write down your answer. How far is it different from your view of wisdom?

KEY WORDS

bodhisattva   sutra   Prajna   Sunyata

THE LOTUS SUTRA

The Lotus Sutra (the Lotus of the True Law or Saddharmapundarika), contains what is thought by Mahayana Buddhists to have been the final teaching of the Buddha.

Like all good teachers, the Buddha was able to adapt his teaching to suit the level of understanding of his listeners. This ability, known as upaya or 'skill in means', is explained in the Lotus Sutra:

Tibetan monks debating the scriptures. It is a traditional technique to test each other's knowledge

I preach the Dharma to all beings
    whether their intellect
Be inferior or superior, and their
    faculties weak or strong...
When I rain down the rain of the
    Dharma
Then all this world is well refreshed
Each one according to their power to
    take to heart.

The Lotus Sutra explains that there are different vehicles or teachings which are used by the Buddha to help and encourage the faithful to Perfect Buddhahood. In reality, however, there is only one vehicle, the Buddha vehicle, which takes the path of the Bodhisattva Mahasattva or Great Being.

This idea is explained in the parable of the Burning House. A father uses the reward of favourite toys: bullock, goat and deer carts, to entice his children out of a burning house. Once outside and safe, the children find that the toys are identical. The action of the father is like the skilfulness of the Buddha.

Then the man gave to each child a bullock cart only, beautifully decorated. He did so because he rightly thought 'Why should I give them inferior carts? I ought to treat all my children equally.' The Buddha is not guilty of falsehood when he first speaks of three vehicles and then leads all to complete Nirvana by just one great vehicle – the Buddha

Vehicle.... Unless they are forced to leave the triple world, which is like a house on fire, how are they to get acquainted with Buddha knowledge?

The bodhisattva path

By striving to possess the qualities of a bodhisattva, lay Mahayana Buddhists, as well as monks and nuns, are able to achieve Perfect Buddhahood. A Mahayana Buddhist explained:

'The first step is to aspire towards perfect wisdom and compassion by taking the Bodhisattva Vow:

To save all beings from difficulties
To destroy all evil passions
To learn the truth and teach others
To lead all beings towards
    Buddhahood.

We then continue along the bodhisattva path by practising the Six Perfections: patience, giving, morality, vigour, meditation and wisdom.'

ASSIGNMENTS

● Try to explain the words 'patience' and 'giving' to three children, aged five, nine and 16. Write down what you would say in each case. Use your 'skill in means'. Use this experience to help explain why this quality is thought to be such an important one in the Lotus Sutra.

FROM THE PEN TO THE HEART

When Buddhism reached China and Japan, two new schools of thought developed: the Pure Land School and Ch'an or Zen School.

Pure Land Buddhism

The two Sukhavativyuha Sutras, which were written in the second century CE, describe a pure land or Sukhavati free from suffering and unsatisfactoriness. Sukhavati is not an actual place but a spiritual realm created by the Buddha himself. Here, with his bodhisattvas, he creates conditions that help spiritual progress take place. It is **Sukha**, the opposite of Dukkha, and is found within the hearts of those aspiring to Perfect Buddhahood. These scriptures describe this Pure Land as:

> a world called Sukhavati (a happy country) where there is neither bodily nor mental pain for living beings. The sources of happiness are innumerable.

During the fifth and sixth centuries the Sukhavativyuha Sutras became responsible for a cult which developed in China and Japan. It is a Buddhism of faith which revolves around the Pure Land of the Buddha Amitabha. (He is known as Amida in Japan.) Amitabha is the Buddha of Infinite Light and Compassion. All who wish to be reborn into his Pure Land have only to call his name 10 times at the time of death and he will appear and escort them to his Sukhavati. In the present world sphere, or Saha, it is difficult to become enlightened but here they will be helped along the path towards Nirvana.

Ch'an and Zen Buddhism

In the sixth century an Indian monk, Bodhidharma, founded a meditation or Ch'an sect in China. He believed that many monks were becoming too attached to the scriptures and he aimed to return to the basic teachings of the Buddha. For him the secret of enlightenment ('satori' in Japanese) was in the nature of one's own heart, but constantly hidden by hatred, craving and ignorance.

By the twelfth century these ideas had reached Japan and became known as **Zen**. Zen transformed everyday activities into meditation practices. If people could purify their minds, then the worldly realm of Saha could become Sukhavati. The scriptures, although important, were not the central feature of this tradition.

Various techniques for meditation developed. Flower arranging, poetry, calligraphy, garden design, archery, the tea ceremony and self-defence became ways of developing mindfulness. Monks also devised riddles or **koans**. Here is an example: 'What is the sound of one hand clapping?' Koans had no logical answer, but encouraged wisdom and sought to transform the nature of the heart.

ASSIGNMENTS

● This is the head of a huge statue of Amida Buddha in Kamakura. Imagine that you are a Buddhist tourist guide in Japan. Outline the importance of this statue to a non-Buddhist tourist.

● Turn back to page 12 and read the parable of the Raft. Explain the link between the parable and the Zen view of scriptures.

● Find another Zen koan. Explain how this is meant to help a Zen Buddhist gain understanding.

KEY WORDS

Sukha   Zen   koan

'Adoration to Amitabha,
Adoration to him whose
soul is endowed with
incomprehensible virtues.'
[Larger Sukhavativyuha Sutra]

HUSTLE AND BUSTLE

● Look carefully at the picture below. Write down some of the things you see.

Did you write down the bee on the daisy? It is probably not on your list as you were too busy looking at the child. Our minds are like this. They are constantly buzzing with activity, full of questions and decisions: What time is it? What shall I wear? Where did I leave my school bag? Now look closely at the picture opposite. How often do we look that closely at ourselves or the world around us? How often do we find the time to be peaceful and calm?

● Just sit still and be quiet for a moment. What can you hear? On your way home try to hear the birds singing. This will involve concentration as our world is full of noise.

What is meditation?

The aim of **meditation** is to help remove all the hustle and bustle from our minds so that we can see things more clearly.

The Buddha taught that through the practice of meditation it is possible to remove greed, hatred and ignorance and to develop other qualities such as peace, tranquility, awareness and insight. This will ensure our harmony with nature and the world around us.

Read the poem below. It is used by Buddhists to introduce young children to meditation practice:

In my room I close the door
Cross my legs and fold my hands
And sit upon the floor.
All is quiet in the house
Just my breath goes in and out
As softly as a mouse.
Ssh! There is nothing now to hear
Then suddenly the voice of silence
Bursts upon my ear.

You can see that the poem gives simple instructions about the way to sit and what to do. It is not always necessary to sit cross-legged but it is important to sit comfortably. Most people, however, find the lotus position gives the best support to the body. It is formed by each foot being placed, sole upward, on the thigh of the opposite leg.

An alternative is the half lotus where the left foot is on the floor under the right leg, and the right foot is on top of the left thigh.

● Try sitting in one of the cross-legged positions and see if you can concentrate on your breathing. Try it for three minutes and then share your experience with a partner. Is it easy or difficult?

'Quieten your mind. Reflect. Watch.'
[Dhammapada 24]

ASSIGNMENTS

● You have been asked by a local radio station to produce a 60-second speech outlining meditation practice. Write the speech.

● Give three reasons why today's society could benefit from meditation practice. Write these down with an explanation for each one.

KEY WORDS

meditation

CALMNESS AND TRANQUILITY

The poem on page 32 draws attention to the breath going in and out. This type of meditation practice encourages calmness and tranquility. It is called **samatha** meditation. It is concentration on an object, like the breath. It can be done while walking, as in the photograph.

● You might like to try this. Measure a distance of about 25–30 paces. Make this your meditation path. Stand at one end of the path and begin walking slowly and carefully, keeping your eyes about three metres in front of you. As you walk, direct your attention to your feet and see if you can feel each bone as it touches the ground. Become aware of your foot and the way it moves.

The four sublime states

Once you have managed to focus your attention on the body, you could take samatha meditation one stage further and meditate upon one of the four sublime states, or **Brahma Vihara**:

metta – loving kindness
karuna – compassion
mudita – sympathetic joy
upekkha – equanimity/serenity

● Try this example of metta meditation. Sit down in a quiet place for 15 minutes. Concentrate on your breathing to help you relax. Let thoughts just pass through your mind. Do not follow them or hold them there. Be peaceful, calm and content, and then read the following passage very slowly or continually repeat the first line.

May all beings be happy and secure; may their minds be contented. Whatever living beings there may be – feeble or strong, long or tall, stout or medium, short, small or large, seen or unseen, those dwelling far or near, those who are born and those who are yet to be born – may all beings, without exception, be happy minded! Let not one deceive another nor despise any person whatever in any place. In anger or ill will let not one wish any harm to another. Just as a mother would protect her only child even at the risk of her own life, even so let one cultivate a boundless heart towards all beings. Let one's thoughts of boundless love pervade the whole world – above, below and across – without any obstruction, without any hatred, without any enmity.

[Metta Sutta]

ASSIGNMENTS

● Search through your music collection. Make a list of the pieces that you find relaxing and calming. Play one or two and write down the things that come to your mind.

● Using the example given for metta meditation, see if you can write a poem or short piece of prose for upekkha meditation.

● What changes are likely to take place if each member of your class began this type of meditation practice? Discuss this and then write a short explanation of your views.

KEY WORDS

samatha   Brahma Vihara   metta
karuna   mudita   upekkha

THE CLEAR POOL

Try to be mindful, and let things take their natural course. Then your mind will become still in any surroundings, like a clear forest pool. All kinds of wonderful, rare animals will come to drink at the pool, and you will clearly see the nature of all things. You will see many strange and wonderful things come and go, but you will be still. This is the happiness of the Buddha.

This Thai Buddhist monk is saying that the mind is like a pool and once you have calm, still water it becomes possible to look beneath the surface.

Once you have calmed the mind using an object such as the breath, it then

becomes possible to stand back and let the mind watch this mental development taking place.

Our thoughts are experiences which come and go. The mind also has qualities of Dukkha, Anicca and Anatta. You can no longer say 'I am angry' because the 'I' does not exist. Instead you say 'There is anger in the mind.' Now you can let this anger go and replace it with thoughts of love or kindness.

Buddhists say that as insight meditation develops so does a sense of responsibility towards others.

Truly wisdom springs from meditation.
Without meditation, wisdom wanes;
having known these two paths
of progress and decline
let one conduct oneself
so that wisdom may increase.

[Dhammapada 20]

ASSIGNMENTS

● Using your knowledge and understanding of meditation, explain the quotation that begins 'Truly wisdom springs from meditation.'

● Meditation practice is sometimes regarded as escaping from the problems of the world. Imagine that you are a Buddhist. Write a dialogue about this with a non-Buddhist.

KEY WORDS

vipassana

Mental development

The word 'meditation' originally meant mental development. In vipassana it

WORSHIP?

● Sometimes when you visit a friend or relative you take a gift with you such as flowers. Think why you do this and share your reasons with the group.

Buddhists do not worship in the same way that Christians worship God. Ajahn Anando explains:

'Usually the word "worship" implies it is directed at an external agent. This is not taught in Buddhism. The ceremonies that are performed are ideally to bring about an uplifting, tranquil and insightful state of mind.'

● Look at the picture. Can you see what the pilgrims are offering?

Reverencing the Buddha we offer
    flowers,
Flowers that today are fresh and sweetly
    blooming.
Flowers that tomorrow are faded and
    fallen.
Our bodies too like flowers will pass
    away.
Reverencing the Buddha we offer candles.
To him who is the light, we offer light.
From his greater lamp a lesser lamp we
    light within us.
The lamp of **Bodhi** shining within our
    hearts.

Reverencing the Buddha we offer
    incense,
Incense whose fragrance pervades the
    air.
The fragrance of the perfect life, sweeter
    than incense,
Spreads in all directions throughout the
    world.

To 'revere' someone is to regard them as sacred or to hold them in deep affection. Did you use the word 'affection' or something similar in your reasons for taking flowers to a friend? The Buddha is not regarded as a god, but more as a friend or teacher. The flowers, candles and incense are offered as a gift.

Better even than tending in the forest
A sacred flame for a hundred years
Is one moment's reverence
For the man who has conquered
    himself.
To revere such a man
A master old in virtue and holiness
Is to have victory over life itself.

[Dhammapada 8]

Ajahn Anando uses the word 'ceremonies' to describe the actions that take place. We shall now look at other actions that help to bring about this uplifting, tranquil and insightful state of mind.

ASSIGNMENTS

● Design a poster to go with the verses from the offering ceremony.

● Imagine that you are a Buddhist. Try to explain the meaning of these verses to a non-Buddhist friend. Note that the word 'Bodhi' means 'enlightenment'.

● You have been given the task of interviewing a woman in the photograph about Buddhist 'worship'. Write a list of questions and the woman's reply explaining how the word 'worship' as we use it is incorrect from a Buddhist point of view.

KEY WORDS

Bodhi

Pilgrims at Bodhgaya, the place where the Buddha attained Enlightenment

BODY, SPEECH AND MIND

In Tibetan meditation practice various techniques are used to transform ordinary body, speech and mind into the body, speech and mind of a Buddha. If you look at the photograph you will see that the Tibetan pilgrims are all using different body movements, some are standing, some kneeling, some bowing and others are lying face down on the ground. Each movement or gesture is carried out

Tibetan Buddhists on pilgrimage in Lhasa, Tibet

mindfully to help remove pride, conceit and selfishness.

Bowing

> As long as bowing lasts, Buddhism will last.

● Lie face downwards on the floor with your arms stretched out in front of you. What feeling does it encourage?

This movement is what Tibetan Buddhists call the grand prostration. The number of grand prostrations recommended is 100,000. Can you think why this number should be so large? How many times can you do this movement before it becomes a great effort?

Not all Buddhists practise the grand prostration but they all bow. This outward sign is said to harmonise the body and the mind and it should be done correctly, kneeling and taking the forehead all the way to the floor. If this is not possible then it should be a bow from the waist, or three bows to represent the Buddha, the Dharma and the Sangha.

> Don't make the mistake of watching how others bow. People can be difficult to train. Some learn fast, but others learn slowly. Judging others will only increase your pride. Watch yourself instead. Bow often, get rid of pride.

Mudras

As you can see from the photograph, bowing is accompanied by hand gestures. These are called **mudras** and they have deep symbolic meaning. Tibetan Buddhists use many different mudras to symbolise events and qualities from the lives of Buddhas and bodhisattvas. The one that you see some of the pilgrims in the photograph making is the anjali mudra, the gesture of respect.

The anjali mudra is used by all Buddhists. It is made by placing the palms together directly in front of the chest with the fingers together pointing upwards, although in the Tibetan tradition the palms are sometimes left slightly apart to represent a lotus bud. In Zen Buddhism the anjali mudra accompanies a bow and it is called 'making gessho'. It acknowledges the Buddha nature within all other beings.

ASSIGNMENTS

● Can you think of a gesture to represent friendship? Include it in a sequence of gestures to welcome someone into your home. Try to harmonise your mind and body so that the movements flow together as one ritual. Write an explanation of your ritual.

● 'As long as bowing lasts Buddhism will last.' Imagine someone asked you why Buddhists bow. Give an explanation from a Buddhist point of view.

KEY WORDS

mudra

HEARING CLEARLY

I was once asked the question 'Why do Buddhist monks spend so much time chanting?' See if you can find the answer in this story:

A Western monk had asked to stay in a monastery in Thailand in order to develop his meditation practice. Several days later the Abbot announced that the chanting of the sutras would take place from 3.30 to 4.40 a.m. and from 5.00 to 6.00 p.m.

The Western monk was not happy at this suggestion and he began to argue loudly that he had come to practise meditation and not to waste time chanting. The Abbot then explained to him calmly that real meditation was to do with attitude and awareness in any activity and not just seeking silence in a forest.

● What was it that the Western monk had not understood?

Chanting

For many voices to blend together as one requires concentration. You have to listen carefully to follow, keeping the same tempo, pitch and speed.

● Find a sentence in a book. Now try to say that sentence in unison with a partner. Was it easy? Now join with two others and try the same exercise again.

Here is an example of a Pali chant for you to try (ṁ is pronounced like 'ng') but try the English translation first:

Buddhaṁ saranaṁ gacchami.
Dhammaṁ saranaṁ gacchami.
Sanghaṁ saranaṁ gacchami.
To the Buddha I go for refuge.
To the Dhamma I go for refuge.
To the Sangha I go for refuge.

Mantras

A **mantra** is a sacred sound that creates a special power when it is recited over and over again. It is a sound that comes from within the person and it is used to aid meditation. The best-known mantra is the Tibetan OM MANI PADME HUM, the mantra of the Bodhisattva Avalokiteshvara. The closest translation is 'jewel lotus' but it is often interpreted as 'Hail to the Jewel in the Lotus'.

Sometimes these sayings are written on pieces of paper and placed into prayer wheels like the one in the picture. As the wheel turns so spiritual power is released. The wheels or cylinders are found in various shapes and sizes. Some are small enough to hold in the hand and turn while reciting the mantra.

ASSIGNMENTS

● Make a list of activities where chanting is used to prepare the mind for activity, for example in sport.

● Using your list, explain the importance of chanting as a technique for developing harmony between body, speech and mind.

● Explain what you think might be a difference in purpose between Buddhist chanting and the chanting you have listed above.

KEY WORDS

mantra

Prayer wheels in Bhutan.
Butter is being placed as an offering

SEEING CLEARLY

● Do you ever day-dream? Sit quietly and close your eyes for a moment. See if you are able to create a picture or an image, perhaps of a friend. Now try to visualise details, the colour and shape of the eyes, the hair, the shape of the mouth, nose and chin.

Usually these pictures just come and go in our imagination. They are not held on to or controlled. In Tibetan meditation the practice of visualisation aims to direct and develop these images.

The image is constructed at the start of meditation and then held to stop the mind wandering. This may be for only a few seconds at first but with practice it will gradually increase.

Thangka

A **thangka** (pronounced 'tankah') is a hanging picture which is used for visualisation. The painters are often lay Buddhists who regard this work as a religious activity. Working under the supervision of a monk they create a central design, usually a Buddha or a bodhisattva, on which to focus the concentration.

As one's skill develops it becomes possible to visualise a three-dimensional figure and eventually to transform one's own mind into the mind of the Buddha or bodhisattva.

Often a chant or explanation will accompany visualisation since the words help to aid the concentration. Here is an example of one on the Bodhisattva Chenrezig:

Visualise Arya Chenrezig dissolving into oneself and all sentient beings. One's own body, speech and mind and that of all others become inseparable from the body, speech and mind of Arya Chenrezig.

[Chenrezig Sadhana]

Mandalas

The monks in the picture are making an intricate design with coloured sand. This is called a **mandala** (which means 'circle') and it is often used as the central design for a thangka. It consists of a series of symmetrical patterns that revolve around a central axis. The patterns become a sacred space in which a spiritual journey can take place.

Mandalas are also used in visualisation practice. Adrian, a Tibetan Buddhist, explains:

'Visualisation is the heart of Tibetan Buddhist meditation practice. It helps to control the mind. Mandalas assist the imagination. As you visualise travelling to their centre so you are drawn to the centre of yourself. In the thangka we become the bodhisattva in our mind, transforming our ordinary mind into a mind with the qualities of enlightenment. Mudras and mantras often accompany visualisation as it becomes natural to adopt (or to visualise yourself adopting) the gestures in which that bodhisattva is shown.'

ASSIGNMENTS

● Try to make your own mandala. Find a square piece of paper and divide it with pencil lines as in the diagram below. Draw a symbol at the centre to represent something or someone special to you. Starting from the centre, build up your own pattern and allow your mind to go on a journey through the shapes you create.

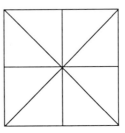

● Compose a poem about your mind's journey called 'Mind Travel'.

● Plan and prepare a talk to the class explaining the value of visualisation practice to a Tibetan Buddhist. Use any visual aids that you think might be useful.

KEY WORDS

thangka   mandala

PILGRIMAGE

A SPECIAL JOURNEY

A pilgrimage is a journey with a special meaning. It can be an outward journey to a sacred place as an act of religious devotion, or an inner journey through life in preparation for a future life.

● Many of us have a place that is special. Perhaps it is a town or even a room in your home. Think for a moment about a place that is special for you. Why is it special?

An outward journey

During his lifetime the Buddha gave his followers four special places that they should visit on pilgrimage:

> If the faithful ... go to the four holy places, they should go and remember; here at Lumbini the enlightened one was born; here at Bodhgaya he attained enlightenment; here at Sarnath he turned twelve wheels of the Dhamma; here at Kushinagara he entered Parinibbana. Bhikkhus, after my passing away there will be activities such as circumambulation of these places and prostration to them.

On the death of the Buddha his body was cremated and divided into eight portions. Four of these went to the places mentioned above, and the remaining four were sent to places that the Buddha had blessed during his lifetime: Rajgir, Shravasti, Sankashya and Nalanda. Over each portion was built a **stupa**, or burial mound, which was the custom at the time.

The great Emperor **Ashoka** (268–233 BCE) was originally opposed to Buddhism but later became a devoted follower and Buddhist ruler. He visited all these sites and at each one erected a great pillar to show its importance. Later he subdivided the Buddha's relics and built thousands of stupas throughout India, giving pilgrims a rich selection of sites to visit.

Until fairly recently these ancient shrines had become overgrown or buried. Pilgrims would have required exceptional strength and the ability to endure extreme loneliness and physical hardship to make the journeys across difficult country. Lumbini itself was only accessible on an elephant. It is not surprising that the Thai word for pilgrimage is 'thudong', stemming from a Pali word meaning harsh or austere practice.

Today, with a growing interest in Buddhism and the help of records left by these pilgrims, archaeologists have begun to excavate and identify these shrines. Once again Ashoka's pillars are visible to pilgrims at Lumbini and Bodhgaya.

For Buddhists living in Britain today, many of these sites are still out of reach but in the next few pages we shall try to capture the atmosphere of a pilgrimage by listening to those who have already travelled the pilgrim path.

ASSIGNMENTS

● Look back at the photograph of pilgrims at Bodhgaya on page 39. What do you imagine the boy on the right is thinking? Write it as a prayer or a poem.

● Imagine that you are a Buddhist able to visit the four main sacred sites while on holiday in India and Nepal. Plan and describe the highlights of your journey, showing your knowledge and understanding of why these sites are important to you. You could use some of the books listed on page 64 to help you.

KEY WORDS

stupa   Ashoka

The Dhamekh Stupa at Sarnath in India

THE BODHI TREE

The ruins at
Anuradhapura in Sri Lanka

By royal request of King Devanampiyatissa to have an order of nuns established in Sri Lanka, King Ashoka sent Princess Sanghamitta with a southern branch of the **Bodhi tree** to Sri Lanka. Being a sacred tree, the king had to make a resolution so that the branch of the Bodhi tree would break away of its own accord. Then the king had it placed in a golden vase that had been prepared for the purpose. King Ashoka had such a deep respect for the tree that he raised the sapling and placed it on board the ship, wading into the water up to his neck. King Devanampiyatissa also received it in equally the same manner of respect.

The history of Buddhism in Sri Lanka began with this planting of the Bodhi sapling in Anuradhapura. Two centuries later it had become a great international centre of Buddhism. Called the city of monasteries, Anuradhapura was visited by pilgrims from thoughout Asia and the monks from its monasteries travelled far and wide. Very little remains of the Brazen Palace, Anuradhapura's oldest monastery, but two thousand years ago a pilgrim described it in this way:

In this most beautiful of palaces there were nine storeys, and in each storey a hundred window chambers. All the chambers were overlaid with silver. A gem pavilion was set up in the middle, adorned with pillars consisting of precious stones, on which were figures of lions, tigers and shapes of gods. Within the pavilion, gaily adorned with seven gems, stood a beauteous shining throne of ivory with a seat of mountain-crystal. Costly beds and chairs, according to rank, and carpets and coverlets of great price were spread about. Surrounded by a beautiful enclosure and provided with four gateways, the palace gleamed in its magnificence.

Today Anuradhapura is one of the largest archaeological sites in the world. Towering over the stone remains are stupas, or **dagobas**. The tallest is 120 metres high and its base circumference is more than 300 metres.

The Bodhi tree, planted in the third century BCE, is the oldest historical tree in the world and one of the most sacred sites of Theravada Buddhist pilgrimage.

ASSIGNMENTS

● Rewrite the story of the sacred Bodhi tree being taken to Anuradhapura, for a young child, and illustrate it.

● What does the description of the monastery tell you about the Buddhist Sangha two thousand years ago? Write an entry for a guide book.

● You are a pilgrim in Anuradhapura. Write about your visit explaining the significance of the Bodhi tree.

KEY WORDS

Bodhi tree   dagoba

A LIVING BODHISATTVA

The leader of the world's Tibetan Buddhists is the **Dalai Lama**. 'Dalai' means profound or measureless one. He is said to be a rebirth of the Bodhisattva Avalokiteshvara, or Chenrezig as he is known in Tibet.

When a Dalai Lama dies, a search begins to find his successor from children born shortly after the time of death. As part of this complex operation, children are chosen from those with similar physical features to the dead Dalai Lama. Each child is then given a collection of objects and asked to select those items which belonged to the previous Dalai Lama. If they do this successfully they are thought to have recognised their own possessions and be the rebirth of the previous Dalai Lama.

A forgotten city?

In 1952 the Chinese Army marched into Tibet, replacing the old life with communism. The present Dalai Lama fled to India where he now lives in exile. His home, the Potala Palace in Lhasa, was left untouched as a monument for those pilgrims who are able to find an official Chinese guide willing to take them there. In this account, a journalist describes his visit as he accompanied pilgrims to Lhasa, 3,400 metres up in the mountains of Tibet:

Visitors to Lhasa should make straight for the Jokhang [below the Potala, the most important temple in Lhasa], a focus for the hundreds of pilgrims, who arrive often after weeks or months of trekking. As they approach the city, some of them stop every three or four steps in order to throw themselves on to the ground. It's fairly common for pilgrims to wear gloves to deaden the shock of the fall. So many pilgrims have prostrated themselves outside the Jokhang that the stone square in front of it looks like polished marble.

A Western Buddhist was present at a special celebration of the Great Prayer Festival in Southern India, attended by the Dalai Lama. Here she describes the atmosphere as he talks to pilgrims:

The silence of the crowd was impressive and in many of the intent eyes could be glimpsed a hint of tears. To the monasteries, he said that as they now had fine and beautiful temples, in the future they should concentrate on looking after their bodies and grow more nutritious food. If the time came to return to Tibet, they would have to leave their new temples behind, whereas they could take their healthy bodies with them.

'There is something very special about taking photos of his Holiness: when he smiles . . . you feel as though you are alone with the Buddha himself! Sometimes it makes you forget to press the button!'

ASSIGNMENTS

● Discuss how important you think it is to be permitted freedom of religious belief and practice.

● Find out more about the Dalai Lama and write a short biography outlining his importance for Tibetan Buddhists and his contribution to modern society.

● Imagine that you were a radio journalist listening to the Dalai Lama's speech. Write or tape a commentary explaining its meaning to your listeners.

● Imagine that you were a Tibetan Buddhist able to visit Lhasa on pilgrimage. Write a letter home to a non-Buddhist friend explaining the importance of such a visit for you.

KEY WORDS

Dalai Lama

THE PILGRIM PATH

A novice dressed for pilgrimage

The Japanese island of Shikoku is famous for pilgrimage because of its 88 Buddhist temples. It was the home of a monk called Kukai, who helped to mould Buddhism in Japan. He is better known as **Kobo Daishi**, a name given to him after his death. Kobo means 'to spread widely Buddhist teachings' and Daishi means 'master'. He was converted to Buddhism while in China but returned home to Shikoku and became well known for his ascetic practices in lonely places on the island.

Pilgrims to Shikoku follow the route he is said to have taken: a circular one around the island that has no beginning and no end. The journey is 1,000 miles in length. It takes two months to walk along the rugged coasts, over mountains and through villages, stopping at the 88 temples along the route. It is a long and arduous journey but the pilgrim believes that Kobo Daishi walks with him.

The novice in the photograph is preparing to go on pilgrimage. On his chest he carries his travelling pack of cooking utensils, and in his hand he holds a 'sedge' – a hat made of straw to shade his eyes from the sun or protect him from the rain. He will also take with him a staff. This helps him to climb the mountains and symbolises Kobo Daishi.

You have just travelled an inner journey.

The novice in the photograph is making an outward *and* an inward journey. Outwardly he is going to travel a physical journey, but inwardly he is travelling a different journey. It is not necessarily like your inner journey to the past, but it is a spiritual one that helps him to travel the path towards enlightenment. Just as the journey around the island is circular with no beginning and no end, so the quest is never ending. A Western pilgrim wrote:

> I do not know whether I am any closer to enlightenment...but I know that the attempt is worth the effort. This circuit around Shikoku will pull me back to try again and again. It is a striving that goes on. What is important is not the destination but the act of getting there, not the goal but the going – 'the path is the goal itself'.

ASSIGNMENTS

- How easy would it have been to make your inward journey without the objects to help you? Try to draw your objects in a circle and make your own mandala from them.

- Imagine you are asked to give a talk on the purpose of Buddhist pilgrimage. Look back over the information on pages 46–53. Write or tape your talk, trying to explain how the outward journey helps the pilgrim with his or her spiritual progress.

KEY WORDS

Kobo Daishi

An inward journey

- Find six or seven objects or mementoes from different stages in your life. Arrange them in a circle on the floor. Now walk around your circle pausing at each object. Can you think of a word or phrase that sparks off a memory?

VALUES

DEATH AND DESTRUCTION

> Peace and survival of life on earth as we know it are threatened by human activities which lack a commitment to humanitarian values. Destruction of nature and natural resources results from ignorance, greed and lack of respect for the earth's living things.
>
> [His Holiness the Dalai Lama]

The keynote when exploring Buddhist values is the first five precepts and an awareness of them. (Turn back to page 14 and read them again.) To a Buddhist, refraining from injuring living things requires having loving kindness not only for other humans but for the whole world of living creatures. It is the doctrine of **ahimsa** or non-harming.

Protection and preservation

Many of the early monks lived in the forest and walked to nearby villages in search of alms-food. In times of famine the Buddha allowed them to survive on windfallen fruit but taught the monks to be mindful of the fact that, once eaten, fruit is no longer capable of reproduction. The monks were only to eat fruit if:

1 It was damaged by fire
2 It was damaged by a knife
3 It had been damaged by one's nail

A tree nursery in Sri Lanka run by a Buddhist monk. The children are helping to plant seedlings

4 It was seedless
5 The seeds had been removed.

By awareness of their actions the monks would remain careful about the quantity of fruit they ate. This tradition continues today. (See page 21.) If fruit is provided for the dana meal it is first cut by a knife and the words 'kappiyam bhante' (I am making this allowable) are recited. The Buddha said:

> He who abstains from injury to seed life and plant life . . . abandoning the taint of ill will; with heart free from ill will; he abides having regard for the welfare of and feeling compassion for every living thing; he cleanses his heart of the taint of ill will.
>
> [Anguttara Nikaya 5]

ASSIGNMENTS

● Write a commentary on the Buddha's words, explaining what you think he was trying to teach the monks about protection and preservation.

● Find some newspaper headlines that give examples of people breaking the first five precepts. Use them in an essay to show how today's society might benefit if these precepts were followed by individuals and governments.

● Make a board game to show the value of following the first five precepts in today's society.

KEY WORDS

ahimsa

TALL OAKS FROM LITTLE ACORNS GROW

In the Rain Forest
From the top of the tallest tree
To the subsoil of its roots
Live many lives
That Grow, Cherish and Decay
From which man has always been
But a small part
Of their cycles.

Trees played an important role in the life of Siddhattha:

He was born under a sala tree.
He attained enlightenment under a Bodhi tree.
He died between the sala trees in the sala grove.

The Buddha established rules preventing monks from cutting down trees, damaging plants or even disturbing the soil.

● How many species of nature can you think of that live in the trees? Write down 10 of them.

A famous story tells how a monk cut down a tree to repair his own hut. The tree had been home to a god who begged the monk not to cut the tree down. The monk did not listen and in cutting the tree cut off the arm of the god's son.

The story shows that cutting down a tree was a selfish act. It deprived the birds and other animals of their home.

All creatures great and small

The picture shows just one creature that depends on the tree for its existence. If you were to list them all, the list would be endless. David Attenborough wrote in his book, *Life on Earth*:

It is not difficult to discover an unknown animal. Spend a day in the tropical forest of South America, turning over logs, looking beneath bark, sifting through the moist litter of leaves followed by an evening shining a mercury lamp on a white screen and one way and another you will collect hundreds of different kinds of small creatures. Moths, caterpillars, spiders, long-nosed bugs, luminous beetles, harmless butterflies disguised as wasps, wasps shaped like ants, sticks that walk, leaves that open wings and fly, the variety will be enormous and one of these creatures will almost certainly be undescribed by science.

● With the emphasis on care for the environment, discuss how a knowledge of Buddhism might influence behaviour.

'Oh please be silent, let us lend ears,
so that nature may speak.'

ASSIGNMENTS

● Imagine that your local council is about to destroy four acres of woodland in order to build a large factory. Write a letter to a local newspaper about its decision, using your understanding of Buddhist values.

● One of the items a Buddhist monk can possess is a water-strainer. Look again at the first precept (page 14) then imagine you are a monk and explain the importance of this item as fully as you can.

THE QUARRELSOME QUAILS

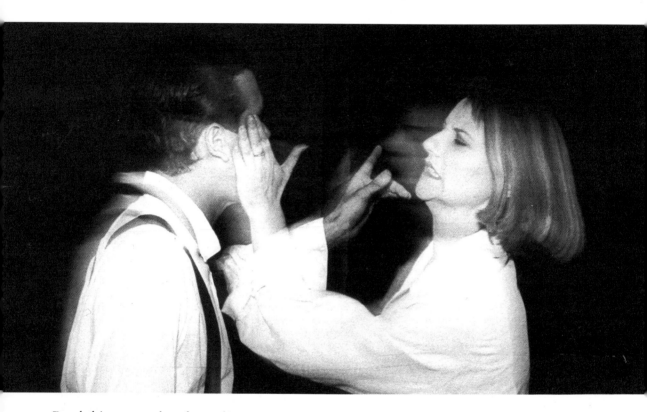

Read this story taken from the
Jataka tales:

'Conquer anger by love and evil by good.'
[Dhammapada 17]

Listen to the cries which pierce the silent forest. They are the cries of six thousand quails. Each day a villager casts a net over them, catching hundreds. One day the King Quail said, 'Cry no more. If you heed your king's words you will never be caught. But if one day quarrels arise and you begin to fight with one another you will be caught and will never see the woods

again.' The quails did as the king advised, and when the net was thrown over them they flew up to the hill with it and escaped.

Each day the villager returned home without a penny. His wife became angry. 'Do not worry,' he said, 'these quails will fight one day.' And so it was. One quail stepped on the head of another and they began to quarrel. Others joined in. 'Let us not stay here,' said the king, 'these unhappy birds will soon come to a bad end.' While the quails went on fighting a dark cloud came over them and they were trapped in the net. The wise king and those who had listened to his teaching were never caught. They lived happily ever after in the silent forest.

● What is the story saying about the Buddha's teaching? Have you ever quarrelled? Could the quarrel have been avoided? Discuss this with a partner and write down some reasons why quarrels begin.

Now read this Zen story on Temper:

A Zen student came to Bankei and complained: 'Master, I have an ungovernable temper. How can I cure it?'

'You have something very strange,' replied Bankei. 'Let me see what you have.'

'Just now I cannot show it to you,' replied the other.

'When can you show it to me?' asked Bankei.

'It arises unexpectedly,' replied the student.

'Then,' concluded Bankei, 'it must not be your own true nature. If it were, you could show it to me at any time. When you were born you did not have it, and your parents did not give it to you. Think that over.'

● Compare this story with the story of the quarrelsome quails. What are they saying about anger?

A human family

Quarrels between two people can cause pain and suffering, but if you look at some newspaper headlines you will see that quarrels between nations and governments result in war, death and destruction. The Dalai Lama in his *A Human Approach to World Peace* wrote:

Whenever I meet even a foreigner
I always have the same feeling
I am meeting another member of the
  human family.
This attitude has deepened
My affection and respect for all beings.
May this natural wish be
My small contribution to world peace.
I pray for a more friendly
More caring and more understanding
Human family on this planet.
To all who dislike suffering
Who cherish lasting happiness
This is my heartfelt appeal.

ASSIGNMENTS

● Do you think it is difficult or easy to 'refrain from false and malicious speech'? Write your own Buddhist story based on this precept.

● Reread the quotation above from the Dalai Lama and write an article for your school magazine explaining Buddhist teaching on world peace.

A STARTING POINT

One of the most important items a Theravada Buddhist monk can possess is the almsbowl. It symbolises the close link between the Sangha of lay people and the monastic Sangha. One cannot exist without the other.

The word 'alms' means gift or donation, and since the time of the Buddha, monks have used their almsbowls to collect their daily food (see page 17). In Ajahn Anando's monastery, when a new monk is ordained he is given an almsbowl made of clay and expected to keep that bowl unbroken for five years. It should be looked after as if it were the head of the Buddha himself. At the time of the Buddha, almsbowls were often broken and so the Buddha made a list of rules to help the monks look after them.

An almsbowl should not be put directly on the ground without protection.
An almsbowl should not be left near the edge of a table or shelf where it may fall off and break.
An almsbowl should be kept in a place where it will not get accidentally knocked over.
An almsbowl should not be scraped with a spoon when eating, or when cleaning it.
No one should open a door with the same hand as they are using to hold an almsbowl (in case someone comes through and knocks it out of their hand).

'Gathering nothing, storing nothing.
Their food is knowledge.
They live upon emptiness.
They have seen how to break free.'
[Dhammapada 7]

An almsbowl should be washed with great care, and should be held in the lap when being dried (in case it slips out of the hands).

Mindfulness

● Look at the photograph. What type of society does it reflect? Can you see any reason why Buddhists in Thailand still feel it is important for their young people to spend some time in a monastery?

The Buddha understood that if the monks could learn to be really mindful about their almsbowls they would extend this to everything else in the universe. The almsbowl was simply a starting point.

Through Buddhism
We shall seek the Truth
Through Ourselves
We must understand
Through Nature
We shall live in harmony
Through our land
Man and Nature flourish in peace.

ASSIGNMENTS

● Make a list of values that you think are important. Write a short piece explaining how they are similar to or different from Buddhist values.

● Write a paragraph or draw a picture to illustrate the meaning of the final quotation that begins 'Through Buddhism'.

● Compose a poem that you think reflects what is valuable about Buddhist teaching and practice.

Glossary

(P) = Pali; (S) = Sanskrit, see page 2

ahimsa The principle of non-injury to living things

Anatta No permanent self

Anicca Non-permanence

Ashoka Indian emperor of 3rd century BCE. He was responsible for Buddhism flourishing in India

bhikkhu (m) bhikkhuni (f) Usually translated 'monk', it originally meant almsman

Bodhi Enlightenment or awakening

bodhisattva A being with the 'essence' of enlightenment

Bodhi tree Mythological name meaning 'Enlightenment' tree

Brahma Vihara The four sublime states

Buddha An enlightened or awakened one

dagoba Buddhist relic monument in Sri Lanka

Dalai Lama Title given to the leader of Tibetan Buddhists

dana Literally 'giving', only meal of the day for Theravada Buddhist monks

Dhamma (P) Dharma (S) The doctrine or teaching of the Buddha

Dukkha The first Noble Truth – unsatisfactoriness

Enlightened A state of perfect understanding

Five Hindrances Major obstacles on the way to enlightenment

Four Noble Truths Core of Buddhist teaching: Dukkha, Samudaya, Nirodha and Magga

Hinayana 'Inferior' or 'Lesser Vehicle', a derogatory term for Theravada Buddhism

karuna Compassion

khandhas (P) skandhas (S) The five elements of being which make up a person

koan Word puzzle or riddle used to create awareness in Zen Buddhism

Kobo Daishi Buddhist monk who helped in the formation of Buddhism in Japan

Magga The fourth Noble Truth, the Middle Way of the Noble Eightfold Path

Mahayana 'Great Vehicle', Northern School of Buddhism

mandala Literally 'circle', a diagrammatic form used in meditation

mantra Sacred syllable or sound

meditation Mental contemplation

metta Loving kindness

mudita Sympathetic joy

mudra Symbolic hand gesture

Nibbana (P) Nirvana (S) Without craving; the highest possible happiness; liberation from the cycle of rebirth

Nirodha The third Noble Truth – letting go of suffering

Noble Eightfold Path The fourth Noble Truth – the prescription for ending suffering and unsatisfactoriness

Parinibbana (P) Parinirvana (S) Complete entry into Nibbana

Prajna Wisdom

precepts Moral instructions or commitments

sadhu A holy man

samanera Literally 'child of a samana' (a religious seeker), a novice monk

samatha A state of inner peace as a result of meditation

Samsara Endless cycle of life, death, rebirth

Samudaya The second Noble Truth – origin of suffering

Sangha The Buddhist community

Siddhattha Gotama (P) Siddhartha Gautama (S) Personal name of the founder of Buddhism

stupa Burial mound often erected over relics of a great Buddhist

Sukha Satisfactoriness or bliss

Sunyata Emptiness

sutta (P) sutra (S) Thread or single idea

Tanha Thirst, craving or desire

Ten Perfections Qualities that lead to perfect Buddhahood

thangka Hanging scroll or picture with religious scenes or symbols

Theravada Doctrine of the 'way of the elders', Southern School of Buddhism

Three Marks of Existence Three aspects of unsatisfactoriness

Three Refuges, Three Jewels The basic Buddhist commitment to the Buddha, Dhamma and Sangha

Tipitaka The three-fold collection of scriptures of the Pali Canon

upekkha Serenity

Vinaya Discipline or rules for life

vipassana Insight meditation

Zen School of Buddhism which developed in Japan

Index

Further reading

Brown, A., J. Rankin and A. Wood. *Religions*, Longman, 1988

Connolly, P. and H. Connolly. *Religions through Festivals: Buddhism*, Longman, 1989

Khan, Noor Inayat. *Twenty Jataka Tales*, East-West Publications, 1975

Landaw, J. and J. Brooke. *Prince Siddhartha*, Wisdom Publications, 1984

Morgan, P. *Buddhism in the Twentieth Century*, Hulton, 1984

Morgan, P. *Buddhist Iconography* and *Buddhist Stories* (both available from Peggy Morgan, Westminster College, North Hinksey, Oxford OX2 9AT)

Morgan, P. *Dictionaries of World Religions: Buddhism*, Batsford, 1987

Naylor, D. and A. Smith. *Buddha: A Journey*, Macmillan, 1987

Rahula, W. *What the Buddha Taught*, Gordon Fraser, 1959

Thompson, M.R. *Buddhist Teaching and Practice*, Edward Arnold, 1985

Acknowledgements

We are grateful to the following for permission to reproduce photographs: Ancient Art & Architecture Collection, page 13 (photo: Ronald Sheridan); © Mohamed Ansar, pages 16, 20, 34; Robin Bath, pages 10, 36; Bruce Coleman, page 57 (photo: P L Fogden); © Mark Edwards/Still Pictures, page 51; Chris Fairclough, page 4; Robert Harding Picture Library, pages 32, 33, 47; Graham Harrison, pages 15, 23, 31, 52; Michael Holford, page 7; © Jimmy Holmes, page 26, Hutchison Library, pages 18, 39, 40 (photo: © Melanie Friend), 43 (© Sarah Errington), 48 (© Bernard Regent); © Greta Jensen, page 44; Brian Mustoe, page 60; Photo Co-op, page 58 (photo: Debbie Humphry), Lois Sayle, page 14; Still Pictures, page 54 (photo: Mark Edwards); Tantra Designs page 46; Merilyn Thorold, page, 25; Lilian Weatherley, pages 8, 9 *above*, 9 *below*.

Cover: Young Buddhist monks reciting mantras in Daklha-Lugug monastery, Lhasa, Tibet. Cepahs Picture Library (photo: Nigel Blythe)

LONGMAN GROUP UK LIMITED
Longman House, Burnt Mill, Harlow,
Essex CM20 2JE, England
and Associated Companies throughout the world.

© Longman Group UK Limited 1992
All rights reserved. No part of this publication may be reproduced, stored in a retrieval system, or transmitted in any form or by any means, electronic, mechanical, photocopying, recording, or otherwise without either the prior written permission of the Publishers or a licence permitting restricted copying issued by the Copyright Licensing Agency Ltd, 90 Tottenham Court Road, London WC1P 9HE.

First published 1992
Second impression 1993
ISBN 0 582 02965 1

Set in 11/14 Garamond
Produced by Longman Singapore Publishers Pte Ltd
Printed in Singapore

The Publisher's policy is to use paper manufactured from sustainable forests.

Additional sources:
J. Snelling, *The Buddhist Handbook*, Century, p. 6; W. Rahula, *What the Buddha Taught*, Gordon Fraser, pp. 6, 19, 23, 24; Ven. Acariya Maya Boowa Nanasampanno, *Straight from the Heart*, p. 8; *The Diamond Sutra*, Buddhist Pub. Group Leicester, p. 27; E. Conye, *The Heart Sutra*, Wisdom Publications, p. 27; E. Conye *et al.*, *Buddhist Texts through the Ages*, Harper & Row, p. 29; E.B. Cavell, *Buddhist Mahayana Texts*, Dover Pub. Inc., pp. 30, 31; Ajahn Chah, *A Still Forest Pool*, Quest, pp. 37, 41; T. Norbu, *Chenrezig Sadhana*, p. 45; J. Russell, *The Eight Places of Buddhist Pilgrimage*, Mahayana Publications, p. 46; J. Mirsky, *Marie Claire* magazine: 'Tibet', November 1988, p. 50; G. Jensen, *Wisdom* magazine, Wisdom Publications, February 1984, pp. 50, 51; O. Statler, *Japanese Pilgrimage*, Picador, p. 53; His Holiness the Dalai Lama, *Tree of Life*, Buddhist Perception of Nature, p. 55; D. Attenborough, *Life on Earth*, Collins/BBC, p. 56; P. Reps, *Zen Flesh, Zen Bones*, Penguin, p. 59

We are grateful to the following for permission to reproduce copyright material: Amaravati Buddhist Centre for extracts from several Amaravati texts © Amaravati Publications, Amaravati Buddhist Centre, Great Gaddesden, Hemel Hempstead, Hertfordshire HP1 3BZ; Alfred A Knopf, Inc for extracts from *The Dhammapada: The Sayings of the Buddha* translated by Thomas Byron, text Copyright © 1976 by Thomas Byron; Pali Text Society for extracts from Digha Nikaya and Dhammapada; Stanley Thornes (Publishers) Ltd and the author, Peggy Morgan, for an extract from *Buddhism in the Twentieth Century* by Peggy Morgan; Wildlife Fund Thailand and the author, Chatsumarn Kabilsingh for extracts from *A Cry from the Forest* by Chatsumarn Kabilsingh, Copyright © 1987 Wildlife Fund Thailand; Wisdom Publications for an extract from *A Human Approach to World Peace* by the Dalai Lama, Copyright © Terzin Gyatso, the Fourteenth Dalai Lama.

Ceremonies and

FEASTS AND FASTING

KERENA MARCHANT

HODDER
Wayland

an imprint of Hodder Children's Books

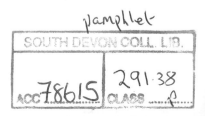

Ceremonies and Celebrations
FEASTS AND FASTING

Other titles in this series are:
BIRTHS • WEDDINGS • GROWING UP
LIFE'S END • PILGRIMAGES AND JOURNEYS

Produced for Hodder Wayland by
Roger Coote Publishing
Gissing's Farm, Fressingfield
Suffolk IP21 5SH, UK

Published in Great Britain in 2000 by Hodder Wayland, an imprint of
Hodder Children's Books

© Hodder Wayland 2000

First published in paperback 2001

Editor: Alex Edmonds
Designer: Tim Mayer

Consultants:
Khadijah Knight is a teacher and consultant on multicultural education and Islam. She is also the author of several children's books about Islam.
Marcus Braybrooke is a parish priest and lecturer and writer on inter-faith relations. He is joint President of the World Congress of Faiths.
Kanwaljit Kaur-Singh is a local authority inspector for education. She has written many books on the Sikh tradition and appears on television regularly.
Sharon Barron regularly visits schools to talk to children about Judaism. She has written two books about Judaism for Hodder Wayland.
Meg St. Pierre is the Director of the Clear Vision Trust, a charitable trust that aims to inform and educate about the teachings of Buddha.
VP Hemant Kanitkar is a retired teacher and author of many books on Hinduism.

The right of Kerena Marchant to be identified as the author of this Work has been asserted by her in accordance with the Copyright, Designs and Patents Act 1988.

Picture acknowledgements
Circa Picture Library 6, 18 (William Holtby); Hutchison Library *front cover* centre right (Nigel Howard), 1 (Nigel Howard), 8 (Nigel Howard), 21 (Juliet Highet), 26 (Patricio Goycoolea), 27 (Liba Taylor), 29 (Nigel Howard); Panos Pictures 28 (Daniel O'Leary); Peter Sanders *front cover* top left, 4, 14, 17; Tony Stone Images *front cover* top right (Leland Bobbe); Trip *front cover* bottom left (H Rogers), 5 (H Rogers), 7 (H Rogers), 9 (H Rogers), 10 (S Shapiro), 11 (H Rogers), 12 (A Tovy), 13 (A Tovy), 15 (C Rennie), 16 (H Rogers), 19 (H Rogers), 20 (Dinodia), 22 (H Rogers), 23 (H Rogers), 24 (H Rogers), 25 (B Dhanjal).

A Catalogue record for this book is available from the British Library.
ISBN 0 7502 3708 2

Printed and bound in Italy by G Canale & C. S.p.A. Turin, Italy

Hodder Children's Books
a division of Hodder Headline Limited
338 Euston Road, London NW1 3BH